JUN   2012

S0-ARG-296

FORCES OF NATURE

Volcanoes

By S.L. Hamilton

Visit us at
www.abdopublishing.com

Published by ABDO Publishing Company, PO Box 398166, Minneapolis, MN 55439. Copyright
©2012 by Abdo Consulting Group, Inc. International copyrights reserved in all countries.
No part of this book may be reproduced in any form without written permission from the
publisher. A&D Xtreme™ is a trademark and logo of ABDO Publishing Company.

Printed in the United States of America, North Mankato, Minnesota.
092011
012012

 PRINTED ON RECYCLED PAPER

Editor: John Hamilton
Graphic Design: Sue Hamilton
Cover Design: John Hamilton
Cover Photo: AP
Interior Photos: Alaska Volcano Observatory-pg 11; AP-pgs 1, 11 (bottom), 26-27, 28 (insert);
Corbis-pgs 4-5, 12-13, 14, 15, 24-25; Getty Images-pgs 7 (top & middle), 10, 16-21, 28-29;
National Geographic-pg 11 (top); NOAA/Natl Geophysical Data Center-pg 6; Thinkstock-pgs
2-3, 6, 7 (bottom), 8, 10 (insert); US Geological Survey-pgs 13, 22 & 23, Wikimedia-pg 14.

ABDO Booklinks
Web sites about Forces of Nature are featured on our Book Links pages. These links are
routinely monitored and updated to provide the most current information available.
Web site: www.abdopublishing.com

Library of Congress Cataloging-in-Publication Data

Hamilton, Sue L., 1959-
  Volcanoes / S.L. Hamilton.
     p. cm. -- (Forces of nature)
  Includes index.
  ISBN 978-1-61783-264-2
  1. Volcanoes--Juvenile literature. I. Title.
  QE521.3.H237 2012
  551.21--dc23

                           2011029673

Contents

Eruption!

Molten rock and gases deep within the Earth are blasted to the surface during volcanic eruptions. Volcanoes can be as explosive as atomic bombs. They are powerful, unpredictable forces of nature.

XTREME FACT – The Volcanic Explosivity Index (VEI) is a scale created in 1982 to measure the explosiveness of a volcano's eruption. The scale runs from a gentle, non-explosive "0" rating up to a mega-colossal "8" rating.

The Science

Deep underground, melted rock (magma) rises through cracks and fissures in the Earth's crust, propelled by pressure and gases. When it reaches the surface, a volcanic eruption occurs. There are four main kinds of volcanoes: cinder cone, composite, shield, and lava dome.

Cinder Cone Volcano
A cinder cone volcano is made of small pieces of hardened lava called "cinders." Parícutin volcano (right) is a cinder cone volcano that erupted in a cornfield in Mexico in 1943.

XTREME FACT – The study of volcanoes is called volcanology. A person who specializes in this study is called a volcanologist.

Composite Volcano (also called Stratovolcano)
Guatemala's Santa Maria has a tall cone made of varying layers of lava, ash, cinders, and other types of rock.

Shield Volcano
Hawaii's Mauna Loa is made of a buildup of lava flowing from a central vent. It has a curved shape like a soldier's shield.

Lava Dome
California's Lassen Peak formed when thick lava cooled over the volcano's vent, giving it a dome-like shape.

Lava vs Ash

When magma is thin and runny, pressurized gases are able to escape through the volcano's vent. The magma then flows down the sides of a volcano as a liquid called lava.

If magma is very thick, gases build up pressure until an explosive eruption occurs. Magma hits the atmosphere and turns into a solid called tephra. Much of it is small ash, but some pieces can be as big as boulders.

XTREME FACT – When melted rock is still beneath the Earth's surface, it is referred to as "magma." Once it hits the surface, it is called "lava."

Historic Eruptions

There are about 1,500 active volcanoes on Earth. Some erupt and are mostly forgotten. Other volcanic eruptions have been so deadly that they are remembered and studied today.

In 79 AD, Italy's Mount Vesuvius violently erupted. The nearby towns of Pompeii and Herculaneum were buried in hot ash, killing thousands. Volcanic Explosivity Index (VEI): 5

In 1912, Alaska's remote Novarupta erupted. The sound was heard 750 miles (1207 km) away in Juneau. It may have been the largest eruption of the 20th century. Volcanic Explosivity Index (VEI): 6

RUSSIA
CANADA
ALASKA
Novarupta

XTREME FACT – Ash from Mount St. Helens fell on 11 states. It was estimated to be enough to cover a football field to a depth of 150 miles (240 km).

In 1980, Washington's Mount St. Helens erupted, killing 57 people and blasting millions of tons of ash into the sky. VEI: 5

Infamous Volcanoes

Earth's volcanoes are found from Iceland to Antarctica. However, about 75 percent are found in an area known as the Pacific Ring of Fire. Tectonic plates, large sections of Earth's crust, slowly move and collide in this area, resulting in many earthquakes and volcanoes.

Hawaii's Mauna Loa is the world's largest active volcano.

Asia

Greenland

RING OF FIRE

North America

Equator
PACIFIC OCEAN

South America

Australia

Eyjafjallajokull

Iceland's Eyjafjallajokull (pronounced ay-yah-fyah-lah-yoh-kuul) is a stratovolcano. In 2010, Eyjafjallajokull spewed an ash cloud to a height of 55,000 feet (16,764 m). Because volcanic ash clogs plane engines, air traffic over Europe was shut down for five days.

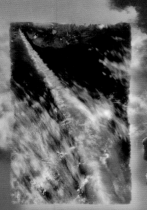

Eyjafjallajokull's ash cloud from space.

Kilauea

Kilauea is a shield volcano whose activity helped create Hawaii's Big Island. Lava both rolls out of the volcano, as well as erupts violently.

Krakatau

In August 1883, Indonesia's Krakatau (also called Krakatoa) went from an island mountain spitting ash and dust to a killer of more than 36,000 people. Its explosion caused most of the island to drop into the sea. Huge sea waves flooded nearby coasts, wiping out whole villages. Today, Krakatau bubbles and boils once again. If it erupts, its devastation would be far greater. Thousands more people live in the area now.

XTREME FACT – Krakatau's 1883 eruption had an explosive force 13,000 times the power of the atomic bomb dropped on Hiroshima, Japan. The explosion was heard 2,200 miles (3,540 km) away in Australia.

Mount Etna

Italy's Mount Etna is the tallest volcano in Europe. It is an active stratovolcano, looming over the city of Catania. Volcanic tremors warn of eruptions of lava and ash. Fueled by bursting gas bubbles within the magma, the lava fountains high into the air.

Nyiragongo

Nyiragongo sits on the eastern edge of the Democratic Republic of the Congo, Africa. It is a stratovolcano with an unusual feature. Inside the main crater is a lava lake. The lake's depth varies from about 2,000 feet (610 m) to a whopping 8,800 feet (2,682 m).

XTREME FACT – In 1977, Nyiragongo's crater walls burst. The lava lake blasted down the volcano's sides, reaching speeds of 60 miles per hour (97 kph). The lava killed more than 70 people.

Mount Pinatubo

In 1991, the Philippines' Mount Pinatubo violently awakened after sleeping for about 500 years. The stratovolcano blasted billions of tons of ash and debris into the atmosphere. Wind blew the debris around the Earth, causing temperatures to drop by an average of .9° Fahrenheit (.5° C).

Pinatubo's ash cloud reached a height of 21 miles (34 k).

More than 700 people died from mud flows, collapsed roofs, and disease.

Lahars (ash mixed with rain) buried whole villages.

Puyehue

Earthquakes awakened Chile's Puyehue volcano in June 2011. Thousands of people evacuated as Puyehue (pronounced poo-yay-way) shot a massive ash cloud into the air for the first time in 50 years. The stratovolcano's eruption closed airports in South America and Australia, and caused high danger alerts for people in the area.

XTREME FACT – Scientists are not completely sure what starts volcanic lightning, but it is often seen in "gray eruptions," ones with lots of ash particles.

Shinmoedake

Blazing hot volcanic ash and rocks billowed out of Japan's Shinmoedake volcano in January 2011. Shinmoedake's blast shattered windows four miles (6.4 km) away. The active stratovolcano's ash closed nearby roads, railroads, and airports.

XTREME FACT – Shinmoedake appears in the 1967 James Bond film You Only Live Twice *as the location of a secret rocket base.*

Surviving an Eruption

The best way to survive a volcanic eruption is to get away BEFORE IT ERUPTS! If trapped, stay indoors. Wear a mask and goggles or cover your face with a cloth to keep ash out of your lungs. Fill a bathtub and sinks with water, in case water stops flowing. Listen for emergency instructions on a radio or other device.

XTREME FACT – In 1902, on the Caribbean island of Martinique, Mount Pelée erupted, killing 30,000 people. One survivor was in a jail cell with poor air flow. Another escaped by boat into a sea cave.

Glossary

Atomic Bomb

An atomic bomb unleashes the energy in atoms, the small particles that make up all matter. An atomic bomb has great destructive power. Some volcanic eruptions release the same amount of energy as 70 atomic bombs.

Herculaneum

An ancient Roman town in Italy destroyed by the volcanic eruption of Mount Vesuvius in 79 AD. Completely buried, Herculaneum was found when a well was being dug in the 1700s. See also Pompeii.

Hiroshima

A city in Japan where the first atomic bomb used in World War II was dropped by the United States on August 6, 1945. The city was destroyed.

Lahar

When volcanic ash and other debris combines with water (such as rain or melted snow on top of a volcano) to create a mudflow or landslide.

Lava Lake

A large amount of lava contained in a volcano's crater. The term may mean liquid lava, or it may mean a lake of lava that has cooled and become solid.

Pacific Ring of Fire

An area around the Pacific Ocean where about 75 percent of the world's most active volcanoes are found.

Pompeii

An ancient Roman town near Naples, Italy, that was buried in ash by the volcanic eruption of Mount Vesuvius in 79 AD. Scientists have been excavating and studying the site since the mid-1700s. See also Herculaneum.

Stratovolcano

A common name for a composite volcano. This type of volcano is made up of layers of ash and lava.

Tephra

Rock fragments ejected from a volcano. The fragments may be as small as ash or as big as a bolder.

Volcanologist

A scientist who studies volcanoes.

Volcanology

The study of volcanoes and volcanic activity.

Index